**A DORLING KINDERSLEY BOOK**

**Written and edited by** Mary Ling
**Art Editor** Helen Senior
**Production** Shelagh Gibson
**Illustrators** Sandra Pond and Will Giles
**U.S. Assistant Editor** Lara Tankel
Special thanks to Windsor Safari Park
Lion and lioness photography page13, Dave King
Zebra photography pages 16/17, Nicholas Parfitt

First American Edition, 1993
2 4 6 8 10 9 7 5 3 1

Published in the United States by
Dorling Kindersley, Inc., 232 Madison Avenue
New York, NY 10016

ISBN   1-56458-311-2
C.I.P. data is available.
Color reproduction by Colourscan, Singapore
Printed in Italy by L.E.G.O.

# SEE HOW THEY GROW
# GIRAFFE

photographed by
## PETER ANDERSON

DK

**DORLING KINDERSLEY**

LONDON • NEW YORK • STUTTGART

# Just born

I was just born.
Phew! It was
hard work. Now
I'll take a nap.

This is my mother.
She takes me to
meet the other
new giraffes.

We play together
while the grown-ups
go and eat.

# Swishy tails

Now I am two
weeks old. Black
tufts of hair are
growing from
my little horns.

I swish my
tail around
when I walk.
Whoosh!

I have a very long
neck which makes
cleaning my
coat easy.

Where is my mom?
I will look for the
special pattern
on her coat.

# Clean ears

Even though I am two
months old, I like staying
close to Mom.

She cleans
behind my
ears because
I can't reach.

Mom shows
me where
to look for
leaves to eat.

11

# Danger, danger!

I am four months old. I am taller and can see far away.

We watch for danger as we graze.

When we see lions
hunting for food,
we move on.

# Tasty treats

I am six months old. My
coat is dark brown
and white now.

Sometimes I drink my
mother's warm milk.
I like grass, too.

Mom likes to reach
up and eat the
tender shoots at
the top of the trees.

# Walk tall

I am eight
months old.
My legs are
long and strong.

I am much
taller than the
little zebras.

Today, the zebras are eating with us.

# A tall story

I am one year old.
My horns are thick.
My hooves are big.
I am so tall I can reach
up to the treetops.

# See how I grew

Newborn   Two weeks old   Two months old   Four months old

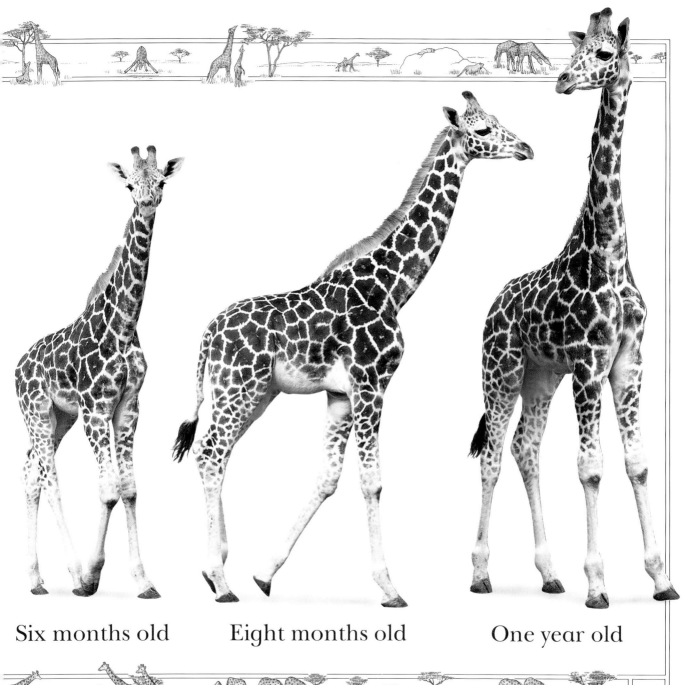

Six months old          Eight months old          One year old